YOU CAN BE A DISCIPLE OF JESUS CHRIST

written by
Jessica Patterson Turner

illustrated by
Nicole Koa

CFI • An imprint of Cedar Fort, Inc. • Springville, Utah

ISBN 13: 978-1-4621-4511-9
ebook ISBN 13: 978-1-4621-4653-6

Published by CFI, an imprint of Cedar Fort, Inc.
2373 W. 700 S., Suite 100, Springville, UT 84663
Distributed by Cedar Fort, Inc., www.cedarfort.com

Library of Congress Control Number: 2023951500

Cover design and interior layout by Shawnda T. Craig

Printed in China

10 9 8 7 6 5 4 3 2 1

Printed on acid-free paper

For Milo, Ezra, and Violet—three tiny
but mighty disciples of Christ.

—Jessica

When Jesus Christ walked the earth,
He called disciples by the sea.
These fishermen were meant for
more. He said, "Come, follow me."

They dropped their nets and followed Him
as He ministered and healed.
They followed His example and tried to do His will.

Jesus called disciples long ago, and He calls disciples now.
Will you choose to follow Him? He has shown you how.

Discipleship begins with faith—faith in Jesus Christ.
Learn about His miracles and His loving sacrifice.

Serve Jesus by serving others. Be His hands here on the earth.
Lift burdens and spread kindness. Help others see their worth.

Watch for those who struggle, those frightened and alone.
Jesus was that way; He helped the lonely to feel known.

Disciples heal the world, one small action at a time.
So find the one who's hurting, then let your light so shine!

FOR DAD

Discover what you're good at, your abilities, your gifts.
Then use those talents wisely to serve and help and lift.

Share what you have with those
in need. Listen and forgive.
Be honest, true, and grateful.
That's just how Jesus lived.

See the good in others.
Love as Jesus does.
See man for who he'll someday
be and not for who he was.

At times it may be hard, but strive to choose the right.
Obey the Savior's loving laws with all your heart and might.

Sometimes disciples make mistakes, whether big or small.
But they repent and try again, and God forgives it all.

As you learn of Jesus, spread
His teachings far and wide.
Share what you know about Him.
Be an example and a guide.

Be His witness always by sharing
truth when others doubt.
Loyalty is really what
discipleship is about.

Take Christ's name upon you. That means to be like Him.
You don't need to be perfect. If you fall, just try again!

Pray to Heavenly Father, for He is a loving God.

He promises to help you hold firmly to the rod.

Jesus wants to help you. He'll give
you strength beyond your own.
Your Savior loves you deeply.
You are cherished; you are known.

His Spirit will be with you as
you walk the narrow path.
Dear disciple, you are
promised all the Father hath.

Jesus Christ is the Good Shepherd.
His disciple, choose to be.

With outstretched arms, He calls to you,

"Come, follow me."